W9-BNT-686

I Know Jesus Loves Me

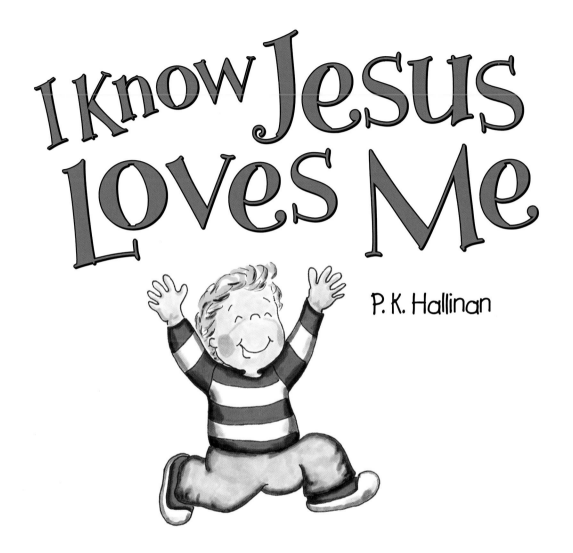

P. K. Hallinan

ideals children's books®

Nashville, Tennessee

ISBN 13: 978-0-8249-5553-3
ISBN 10: 0-8249-5553-6

Published by Ideals Children's Books
An imprint of Ideals Publications
A Guideposts Company
535 Metroplex Drive, Suite 250
Nashville, Tennessee 37211
www.idealsbooks.com

Color separations by Precision Color Graphics,
    Franklin, Wisconsin

Printed and bound in Italy by LEGO

Library of Congress Cataloging-in-Publication Data on file

10 9 8 7 6 5 4 3 2 1

This Book
Belongs to

_____

I know Jesus loves me
In so many ways.
He brightens my nights.

He lightens my day.

Whenever storms come

He's always the one . . .

To push back the clouds
And bring back the sun.

I know Jesus loves me
By the things he creates,
From warm, grassy meadows . . .

To cool, glassy lakes.

His mind has designed
Every creature and flower
To gladden my heart
Every day, every hour.

It's amazing that he
Is always thinking of me.

I know Jesus loves me
By the way he imparts

His goodness and mercy
Right into my heart.

He gives me his grace
So I'll be gentle and fair.

He gives me his kindness
To sow and to share.

He gives me his joy
Till I shine like a beacon,
So others will notice
And wonder and seek him.

Then I simply reveal
What I think and I feel.

I know Jesus loves me
By the way he provides

All that I need
To feel strong and alive!

He fills up my platter
With good food to eat.

He covers my shoulders
And puts shoes on my feet.

He even makes certain,
Every now and again,
To send me a blessing
Just because he's my friend.

It's easy to see
He enjoys pleasing me.

Yes, I know Jesus loves me
By the miracles he shares.
He heals my sad feelings . . .

He answers my prayers.

He loves me so much that he willingly gave
His life on the cross so that I could be saved.

It's a sacrifice too grand
To ever understand.

Yes, I know Jesus loves me,
From my head to my toes;
I feel it inside,
And the Bible says so.

So I'll rest in the shelter

Of my Lord's love so true,

And hope that he notices . . .

I love him too!